INSIDE MLS

CHICAGO FIRE
FC

BY ANTHONY K. HEWSON

SportsZone

An Imprint of Abdo Publishing
abdobooks.com

abdobooks.com

Published by Abdo Publishing, a division of ABDO, PO Box 398166, Minneapolis, Minnesota 55439. Copyright © 2022 by Abdo Consulting Group, Inc. International copyrights reserved in all countries. No part of this book may be reproduced in any form without written permission from the publisher. SportsZone™ is a trademark and logo of Abdo Publishing.

Printed in the United States of America, North Mankato, Minnesota
052021
092021

THIS BOOK CONTAINS
RECYCLED MATERIALS

Cover Photo: Scott Winters/Icon Sportswire
Interior Photos: Jim Ruymen UPI Photo Service/Newscom, 5, 8; Michael Caulfield/AP Images, 7, 17; Mark J. Terrill/AP Images, 11, 41; North Wind Picture Archives, 13; John Swart/AP Images, 15; Patrick Gorski/Icon Sportswire/AP Images, 19; Robin Alam/Icon SMI 164/Newscom, 21; John Raoux/AP Images, 22; Stephen J. Carrera/AP Images, 25; Lee K. Marriner UPI Photo Service/Newscom, 26; Adam Davy/PA Images/Alamy, 28; Nam Y. Huh/AP Images, 31; Graham Hughes/The Canadian Press/AP Images, 32; Aubrey Washington/Allsport/Getty Images Sport/Getty Images, 34–35; Michael S. Green/AP Images, 36; Molly Riley/Reuters/Newscom, 38; Tom Jones/Zuma Press/Newscom, 42

Editor: Patrick Donnelly
Series Designer: Dan Peluso

Library of Congress Control Number: 2020948230

Publisher's Cataloging-in-Publication Data

Names: Hewson, Anthony K., author.
Title: Chicago Fire FC / by Anthony K. Hewson
Description: Minneapolis, Minnesota : Abdo Publishing, 2022 | Series: Inside MLS | Includes online resources and index.
Identifiers: ISBN 9781532194702 (lib. bdg.) | ISBN 9781644945629 (pbk.) | ISBN 9781098214364 (ebook)
Subjects: LCSH: Soccer teams--Juvenile literature. | Professional sports franchises--Juvenile literature. | Sports Teams--Juvenile literature.
Classification: DDC 796.334--dc23

TABLE OF
CONTENTS

WASTING
NO TIME

Jaime Moreno steamed toward the goal. The DC United forward had a golden chance to put his team ahead early. Instead, his shot sailed over the crossbar. The relieved Chicago Fire players looked up at the scoreboard. The match was only 15 seconds old. It could be a long day.

If there was such a thing as a dynasty in a league that was only three years old, DC United was it. The men from the nation's capital won the first two Major League Soccer (MLS) titles. The Fire stood in their way of a third in the 1998 MLS Cup.

The Fire were anything but a dynasty. Chicago was a team in its first year of existence. Just getting to the final was a big accomplishment for such a new team. Most people

Luboš Kubík, bottom, and the Chicago Fire had their hands full against Jaime Moreno and DC United in the 1998 MLS Cup.

expected Chicago's season to end in disappointment against the powerhouse that was DC.

United beat the Fire both times the teams met in the regular season by a combined score of 7–2. Both losses came during two five-match losing streaks the Fire endured. In between those streaks, they won 11 straight matches. The Fire's up-and-down performance made the season unpredictable but exciting.

THE RIGHT MIX

Chicago did not lack talent. Its players may have been new to each other, but fans of world soccer were familiar with them. The Fire had a trio of experienced Polish forwards in Piotr Nowak, Roman Kosecki, and Jerzy Podbrozny. Along with Czech midfielder Luboš Kubík, these players formed the so-called "Eastern Bloc" of Eastern European stars. They were especially popular with Chicagoans of Eastern European heritage.

The Fire also had some young American stars such as midfielder Chris Armas, striker Josh Wolff, and goalkeeper Zach Thornton. In addition, they had a rising coaching star in head coach Bob Bradley. He had been an assistant on DC United's two title teams. All three players would end up

Chicago star Piotr Nowak evades DC United defender Jeff Agoos in the 1998 MLS Cup.

playing for the US men's national team. And Bradley would become the national team's head coach.

DC had its share of talent as well. Eight players and head coach Bruce Arena represented the club in that year's MLS

Fire midfielder Diego Gutierrez dribbles away from DC United forward Marco Etcheverry.

All-Star Game. Arena would be soon be coaching the US men's national team. And United's Eddie Pope and Jeff Agoos had played for the United States in that year's World Cup.

KICKING OFF

The weather conditions for the MLS Cup were perfect. It was a warm and sunny day at the Rose Bowl in Pasadena, California. And United nearly had a perfect start with Moreno's attempt 15 seconds in.

DC kept up the pressure. Its style was to attack. Chicago tried to play solid defense and be prepared to counterattack. For the first half hour, the Fire defense absorbed a lot of pressure. The United players were getting frustrated. They felt the referees were missing calls and Chicago was getting all the breaks.

Chicago was hesitant to send too many players up the field and expose its defense. The Fire carefully and slowly built their attacks. In the 29th minute, their patience paid off. Ante Razov exchanged passes with Nowak near the 18-yard box. Nowak ran free and drew the goalkeeper out to him. At the last second, he passed to Podbrozny, who tapped the ball into a wide-open net.

Chicago doubled its lead just before the half. The Fire took control of the ball in midfield. Nowak carried the ball into the box and cut to the middle. He unleashed a shot that deflected off teammate Diego Gutiérrez and found the back of the net.

EARLY SUCCESS

The Fire were the second expansion team in the major US professional sports leagues to make the championship round in its first season. The St. Louis Blues of the National Hockey League (NHL) reached the Stanley Cup Final in 1968. However, that appearance was something of a fluke. The NHL had doubled in size that season and created a new division composed solely of the six expansion teams. That move guaranteed that one of the six would play in the final.

HANGING ON

United was not going to go away in the second half. But the Fire defense and Thornton kept the potent DC attack contained. Armas was effective at slowing down Marco Etcheverry, the league's Most Valuable Player (MVP) for 1998. Thornton made eight saves.

Kubík and the experienced Fire defense made sure United could not come back. When the final whistle blew, the players flooded onto the field. Nowak leapt into the arms of Thornton in celebration of his shutout. The Fire fans who traveled to the match sang and twirled their scarves in the air.

Hundreds of fans gathered a few days later at Chicago's city hall. Mayor Richard Daley was there to honor the city's newest championship team. But the Fire's season wasn't done yet. In a few days, they would play for another trophy in the US Open Cup final, meaning their already historic season still had more to come.

From left, Piotr Nowak and Jesse Marsch celebrate the 1998 MLS Cup championship.

CHAPTER 2

WINDY CITY
SOCCER

The Great Chicago Fire raged for three days in October 1871. It destroyed one third of the city and left 100,000 people homeless. But Chicago rebuilt its industry through the strength and resolve of its citizens and went on to become a thriving city. That resurrection became a point of pride for generations of Chicagoans.

Many of those people were European immigrants or descendants of the people who had been moving to the city since the 1850s in search of jobs and opportunity. They worked tough and sometimes dangerous jobs in the city's factories and stockyards. They helped shape Chicago into the major city it is today. One of their many contributions to Chicago's culture was soccer.

Chicagoans take pride in the rebirth of their city following the Great Chicago Fire of 1871.

Chicago Sparta was established by Czech immigrants in 1915. The club went on to win the National Challenge Cup in 1938 and 1940. Known today as the US Open Cup, the tournament is open to every men's pro and amateur soccer club in the United States.

Chicago has had other pro soccer clubs over the years. The Chicago Sting played in the North American Soccer League (NASL) from 1975 to 1984. They won the league's Soccer Bowl twice, one of just two teams in NASL history to win multiple championships.

Despite its long history of soccer and a passionate fan base in the other major pro sports leagues, Chicago was not awarded a team for the first season of MLS in 1996. But Chicagoans didn't have to wait too long. The Chicago Fire and the Miami Fusion were announced as the first MLS expansion teams on October 8, 1997. That was 126 years to the day from the beginning of the Great Chicago Fire.

Naming the team after the fire was not the only way the club identified with the city. The Fire also brought in players from Eastern Europe and elsewhere who became favorites in Chicago, one of the most ethnically diverse cities in the country.

Chicago's Soldier Field played host to the opening ceremony for the 1994 World Cup.

The players were popular for more than just where they were from. Piotr Nowak, Luboš Kubík, and Roman Kosecki were all experienced pros from Europe's top leagues. Chicago's coach, Bob Bradley, wanted to bring in veteran players to give the club an early boost. He also identified young and promising players such as Chris Armas and Jesse Marsch.

TROPHY HUNTERS

Chicago proved its roster had just the right makeup when it won the MLS Cup in its first season. And that trophy was no fluke. It wasn't even the only trophy the Fire won that season. Chicago also took the US Open Cup a week later.

The Fire continued their philosophy of mixing experience with young talent. The 2000 team added former Barcelona striker Hristo Stoichkov of Bulgaria and also had a promising American winger in DaMarcus Beasley. That team made it back to the MLS Cup but lost to Kansas City. The Fire did win their second US Open Cup that season, however, as Chicago began to earn a reputation for excellence in that competition.

The Fire were doing everything right and having a lot of success. The one thing the team lacked was a permanent home. The team had played at Soldier Field since 1998. The Fire shared the huge lakefront stadium with the Chicago Bears of the National Football League (NFL).

Soldier Field was way too big for the Fire. It could hold more than 66,000 fans. The Fire averaged crowds of 16,388 in 2001.

Chris Armas, *right*, and Piotr Nowak celebrate Nowak's goal in the 1998 MLS Cup.

Fifty thousand empty seats is not the proper backdrop for a championship team.

And the Bears would always be the main tenant. When Soldier Field needed renovations in 2002, the priority was to interrupt the football season as little as possible. That forced the Fire out for 2002 and 2003. It wasn't until February 2002 that the Fire found a place to play, at Cardinal Stadium on the campus of North Central College in suburban Naperville, Illinois.

After temporary seating was installed, the capacity was only a little smaller than the average Fire crowd. And the Fire's loyal supporters followed the team to the suburbs. The Fire averaged 12,922 fans in 2002 and 14,005 in 2003.

Those fans got to see some history, too. The 2003 regular season was the team's best yet. It posted the best record in MLS and made the MLS Cup. It also won a third US Open Cup. That season also marked the end of an era as it was the first without longtime captain Nowak, who had retired to join the team's front office.

More changes were in store for the franchise. The team's ownership group fired popular general manager Peter Wilt, who had built the Fire's trophy-winning lineups. Not only did he guide the team's success on the field, he also worked closely with its supporters' groups. The Fire had established a strong and passionate fanbase during his time there.

Toyota Park in Bridgeview was built specifically for soccer, giving the Fire a more intimate home.

Wilt's lasting legacy to the club was its first permanent home. His firing came just after Wilt had secured $100 million in funding to build a soccer-specific stadium in suburban Bridgeview, Illinois. Toyota Park opened in time for the club to play the 2006 season in its new home. A fourth US Open Cup title that fall helped make some fond memories right away.

BLANCO'S BRILLIANCE

While the Fire had a reputation for success in the US Open Cup, fans longed for another MLS Cup title. Feeling pressure to win, the club made a big signing for the 2007 season. Cuauhtémoc Blanco had been a big star for Mexico's national team and in the Mexican league. He was a big hit with Chicago's Mexican fans. When the team held an event to announce his signing at Toyota Park, 5,000 fans lined up to get inside.

Fans and teammates loved the attacking midfielder. He was a fiery competitor and hard worker. Even supporters of the US men's national team, Mexico's biggest rival, had to respect how Blanco played. Blanco pushed the Fire to the conference finals in all three seasons he spent in Chicago.

Blanco was not a one-man team. But his departure after the 2009 season coincided with a major downturn for the Fire. Instead of building on their conference finals appearances, the Fire were out of the playoffs entirely in 2010. That began a string of 11 seasons with only two playoff appearances total.

The club did not lack talent. For instance, Mike Magee was named MLS MVP in 2013. But the team just could not find the right combination of players and coaches to build a Cup contender. Andrew Hauptman, who led the team's

Mexican star Cuauhtémoc Blanco helped usher in a new era in Fire history.

ownership group, started to feel the heat. Fans lashed out at his management of the club.

As the Fire limped to an 8–20–6 record in 2015, fans staged protests at Toyota Park. They called for Hauptman to sell the

C. J. Sapong, *left*, and the Fire debuted the team's new identity during the 2020 season.

team. After a few years of declining attendance, fans finally got their wish in 2018. Hauptman sold 49 percent of the team to local businessman Joe Mansueto. The next year, Mansueto bought the rest of the shares and took over the team. By this time, attendance at Toyota Park—since renamed SeatGeek

Stadium—had dwindled to a record-low 12,324 fans per game. SeatGeek Stadium was a great place to watch soccer. But the stadium was hard to get to for most Fire fans in Chicago. And the stadium's neighborhood did not offer many fun activities for before or after the match.

After the 2019 season, the club announced it would be moving back to Soldier Field. The move was controversial. It brought the club closer to more of its fans, but Soldier Field was still an enormous NFL stadium. Most of the successful MLS clubs had long since moved out of those venues. That was not the only controversial move the team made. The Fire also rolled out new colors and a new logo, giving a makeover to the identity the club had spent more than 20 years building. They also traded away veteran players and hired a new coach.

Fans had called for change for years. But with so many significant changes in just a short time, some fans weren't sure how they felt. To make matters worse, the COVID-19 pandemic disrupted the 2020 season and kept fans out of Soldier Field. They could only experience these changes by watching on TV. And on the field, the Fire showed few signs of improvement. However, there was some relief when the team announced after the season that it would again change its crest and visual identity, this time with more fan input.

CHAPTER 3

THE FIREMEN

Even as the Fire passed the 20-year anniversary of their 1998 MLS Cup title, the players who won that trophy remained some of the most-beloved players in team history. Perhaps the most popular of all was Piotr Nowak. He was the first international player the team signed in 1997.

Nowak had been the captain of the Poland national team. Chicago's Polish community was thrilled to see him play in their city. Plenty of other fans loved him, too. Nowak was known as a playmaker. He could score but also excelled at setting up other players for goals. He was a three-time MVP and won the MLS Cup and two US Open Cups with Chicago.

Nowak remains the all-time Fire leader in assists with 48. Ante Razov was on the receiving end of a lot of those passes.

Piotr Nowak set a high standard over his five seasons with the Fire from 1998 to 2002.

Ante Razov proved to be one of the Fire's most reliable scorers over his seven seasons with the team.

Razov became the club's all-time leading scorer and still held the title as of 2021.

Razov averaged a goal nearly every other game, with 76 in 155 games. He played two different stints in Chicago, from 1998 to 2000 and 2001 to 2004. Razov played for four other MLS teams, but he was most identified by his time with the Fire.

THE WINNING TRIO

Only three players were on the field to win every trophy in Fire history. Defender C. J. Brown, midfielder Chris Armas, and goalkeeper Zach Thornton won the 1998 MLS Cup and all four US Open Cup titles.

Brown was on the field more than most. He played for the Fire for 13 seasons. In his career, he appeared in 372 total matches. That includes 296 MLS league games, 35 playoff games, and 25 US Open Cup games. No one in club history has played more minutes or in more games. Brown was the last original Fire player still on the team when he retired in 2010. His hard work and gritty play on defense made

WEARING MANY HATS

Frank Klopas played only two seasons for the Fire, in 1998 and 1999. But that was just one of the roles Klopas has held with the team over the years. He has also worked for the Fire as a trainer, technical director, head coach, and broadcaster. He returned to the Chicago sideline as an assistant coach in 2020.

Goalkeeper Zach Thornton was named the Fire's MVP in 2002 and defender of the year in 2001 and 2002.

him a popular player and teammate. Brown was captain in 2008 and 2009.

Armas formed part of the potent Fire attack with Nowak and Razov. The midfielder spent his first two MLS seasons with the LA Galaxy but played the rest of his career in Chicago. He made four All-Star teams and was Fire captain from 2003 until retiring in 2007. He then became an assistant coach.

Supporting them in goal was Thornton. He saw little playing time with the New York/New Jersey MetroStars. Upon coming to Chicago in 1998, Thornton won the starting job and was named MLS Goaltender of the Year. His 215 games in goal are the most in club history.

INTERNATIONAL STARS

David Beckham gave a boost of star power to MLS in 2007. Another European player made a similar move seven years earlier but didn't get the same headlines. Soccer was still gaining popularity in North America when Hristo Stoichkov signed with the Fire in 2000. Many Americans probably had not heard of him. But he was a star for the Bulgaria national team and for FC Barcelona. Stoichkov was at the end of his pro career but showed he had plenty left to offer. He scored 17 goals in 51 games for the Fire.

Beckham changed everything when he came to the Galaxy in 2007. The league had to change its rules so the English superstar could fit into its salary cap. That created an opportunity for other teams, too. Chicago took advantage of

RING OF FIRE

Chris Armas, C. J. Brown, Frank Klopas, Luboš Kubík, Piotr Nowak, and Ante Razov are all members of Chicago's Ring of Fire. The honor was created in 2003 to recognize legends of the club. Peter Wilt and Bob Bradley also have been enshrined. All Ring of Fire inductees get a say in who is next to join them.

the new rules to sign Cuauhtémoc Blanco. The Mexican national team star was a huge hit on and off the field for the Fire.

Blanco was an attraction all on his own. He was the team's best attacking player in his three seasons. Blanco was an All-Star in 2008 and earned game MVP honors.

By 2008 Brian McBride had put together a historic career. He was the first pick in the first MLS draft in 1996. Then he became one of the first Americans to thrive in the English Premier League, eventually being named captain at Fulham. All the while he also played in three World Cups for the United States, scoring in two of them. After all of that, however, he decided to come home.

McBride grew up in Arlington Heights, Illinois. He was thrilled to finish his career with his hometown team. And the fans were thrilled to have him. McBride teamed with Blanco to give the Fire two proven scorers. McBride chipped in 18 goals

Brian McBride was already one of the most accomplished US men's players when he returned to play for his hometown Fire.

After winning a World Cup as a midfielder for Germany, Bastian Schweinsteiger often played defense during his three seasons with the Fire.

in 59 matches. He retired in 2010 and got a sendoff from the fans in his final home game.

The Fire were hardly done bringing in big-name players, though. Bastian Schweinsteiger made a name for himself in central midfield for much of his legendary career. When he signed with Chicago in 2017, the German national team star did whatever it took to win. That included playing defense.

Schweinsteiger was an integral part of Germany's 2014 World Cup–winning team. Then he helped the Fire make a surprise playoff appearance in 2017. He also served as a mentor to the team's young players. The fans loved him too. Schweinsteiger stayed in Chicago through the 2019 season.

Robert Berić didn't have quite the stature of Schweinsteiger when the Fire signed him in 2020. The Slovenia national team player nonetheless had enjoyed a successful career in Europe and made a big impact in Chicago. Only one player in all of MLS scored more goals in 2020 than Berić's 12.

CARLOS BOCANEGRA

To celebrate the league's 25th season in 2020, MLS named its 25 best players ever. Among them was Carlos Bocanegra. He was named MLS Defender of the Year in 2002 and 2003 while playing with the Fire. He went on to have an esteemed career in Europe and with the US national team.

CHAPTER 4

ETERNAL
FLAMES

The club's name was a secret until October 8, 1997. That was the day the Fire name and logo were unveiled and the club's history began. Less than six months later, players were on the field wearing that name and representing Chicago.

The Chicago Fire played their first game on March 21, 1998, in Miami, Florida. The opponent was the Fusion, who joined MLS the same season. Zach Thornton made some huge saves, including stopping a penalty kick, to keep Miami off the scoreboard. Roman Kosecki finally broke the deadlock with the first goal in Fire history in the 76th minute. Then Ritchie Kotschau doubled the lead in the 87th as the Fire got off to a perfect start.

Roman Kosecki, right, pushes the ball forward against the Miami Fusion in the Fire's 1998 MLS debut.

The Fire celebrate as national champions after winning the 1998
US Open Cup.

More than 36,000 Chicagoans were waiting at Soldier Field
for the Fire's next match two weeks later. In a different time,
Frank Klopas might have been among the crowd in the stands.
Instead, he was on the field playing for his hometown club.

Klopas grew up in Chicago and played for the Sting before spending nine seasons in Greece. He came back to the United States to play the first two MLS seasons with the Kansas City Wizards. He wound up with the Fire in the club's first year, and he helped make their first home opener a memorable one.

Klopas scored two goals that day, the only two of the game against the Tampa Bay Mutiny. They were two of only six goals Klopas would score in two years with the Fire. But Klopas had another big one in him later in the year.

The 1998 season ended magically for the Fire with the MLS Cup title. But the club had another trophy to win just five days later. The US Open Cup final was supposed to be played in Virginia in August. But a hurricane forced a postponement and the match was moved to October at Soldier Field.

Klopas sat on the bench for most of the game against the Columbus Crew. He came on in the 91st minute with the score 1–1. In the 99th minute, Chicago had a corner kick. The ball sailed into the box and Ante Razov headed it towards the goal. Klopas was there. He took a touch and buried a goal with his right foot. Klopas's golden goal for his hometown club won the US Open Cup.

Luboš Kubík and the Fire had the second-best record in MLS in 2000 and made a run to the MLS Cup.

CHICAGO COMEBACKS

In 2000 the already potent Fire lineup got a boost. New signing

Hristo Stoichkov came over from Europe. The team also added

a pair of future US national team stars in Carlos Bocanegra and DaMarcus Beasley. Chicago won its division and began pursuing another MLS Cup.

But its title dreams were hanging by a thread in the semifinals. After splitting the first two games with the MetroStars, Chicago needed a win to advance to the MLS Cup. The Fire built a 2–0 lead but lost it in the first half. Tied at two late, Razov made a run toward goal. Chris Armas saw him and made a perfect pass. One-on-one, Razov beat the keeper for the game-winning goal.

THE BRIMSTONE CUP

The Brimstone Cup rivalry made more sense when FC Dallas was called the Dallas Burn. Chicago and Dallas fans created the cup in 2001 for the two teams with fiery names. The cup has endured even after Dallas changed its name in 2004.

The Fire lost the MLS Cup to Kansas City 1–0 despite firing 10 shots on goal. But a week later, they had a chance to win a second US Open Cup. Just as in the MLS playoffs, the Fire's dreams had almost died in the semifinals. Josh Wolff scored in the 112th minute to secure a win over the LA Galaxy. Then in the final at Soldier Field, Stoichkov scored just before halftime to put the Fire on top. Chicago doubled the lead late in the game and held on to beat the Miami Fusion 2–1 to become two-time US Open Cup champions.

ON TOP OF MLS

The 2003 season was the best in Fire history. The team posted the best record in all of MLS. That earned the Fire the Supporters' Shield trophy.

For the first time, Chicago played a US Open Cup final before the MLS playoffs began. Exciting playmaker Damani Ralph, that year's Rookie of the Year, scored in the final against the MetroStars. That was the only goal Chicago needed as it hoisted a third Open Cup trophy.

But the big prize awaited in the MLS Cup playoffs. After breezing through the conference semifinals, Chicago faced the New England Revolution at Soldier Field. Back home after the stadium was renovated, the big crowd boosted the team's spirits. The hard-fought match was scoreless and went into extra time.

"Captain Chris" Armas was back on the field after missing most of 2002 with an injury. He put together a great season and was MLS Comeback Player of the Year. He completed his comeback by scoring the match-winner in the 101st minute. The Fire did not finish the season with a championship, as a 4–2 loss to the San Jose Earthquakes ended their dreams of

Rookie Damani Ralph and the Fire took the league by storm in 2003.

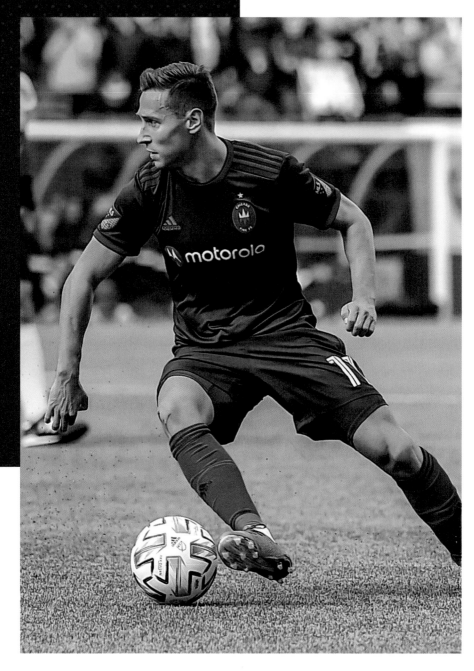

Hopes were high for Przemyslaw Frankowski and the new-look Fire going into the 2020 season.

another double. But Armas's goal remains one of the greatest moments in Fire history.

HELLO AND GOODBYE TO BRIDGEVIEW

The 2006 Fire were homeless for the first nine games of the season. They played on the road until their new suburban stadium was ready. Chicago finally played its first game at Toyota Park on June 11. The first match was a special treat just for the team's loyal season-ticket holders and Bridgeview residents. The invite-only crowd of 12,941 saw Nate Jaqua score two goals in a 3–3 draw with the Revolution.

That 2006 Fire team made the MLS Cup playoffs and won a fourth Open Cup. Thirteen years later, the Fire played their last home game in Bridgeview and almost everything was different. Chicago and Toronto FC each scored two second-half goals for a 2–2 draw on September 29, 2019, at SeatGeek Stadium. The 2019 Fire were 10–12–12 and out of the playoffs.

The Fire left Bridgeview behind along with their original logo and colors. In moving back to Soldier Field and launching a new identity, the club hoped to reignite the passion of its fans and the city of Chicago. Only time would tell if the attempt to rise from the ashes would succeed.

TIMELINE

1997	1998	2000	2003	2004
The Chicago Fire are officially announced as an expansion team on October 8, the 126th anniversary of the Great Chicago Fire that inspired the club's nickname.	The Fire win the MLS Cup and the US Open Cup double in their first season of existence.	Chicago makes another run to the MLS Cup final before losing to the Kansas City Wizards, but it later wins a second US Open Cup.	The Fire wins the Supporters' Shield and a third US Open Cup but loses in the MLS Cup.	Ante Razov retires as the club's leading scorer with 76 goals in regular-season matches and 94 goals across all competitions.

2006	2007	2010	2013	2020
Chicago opens Toyota Park and wins a fourth US Open Cup title in its new home.	The Fire make a splash in signing Mexico national team star Cuauhtémoc Blanco, who leads the team to three conference finals appearances in a row.	Hometown hero Brian McBride, a former US national team star, wraps up his career after a three-year stint with the Fire.	After scoring 18 goals in all competitions, Mike Magee becomes the first Fire player to win the MLS MVP award.	The Fire, sporting a new look, move back to Soldier Field, but fans aren't able to attend games due to COVID-19.

FIRST SEASON

1998

STADIUM

Soldier Field (1998–2001, 2003–05, 2020–)
Cardinal Stadium (2002–03)
SeatGeek Stadium (2006–19)

MLS CUP TITLES

1998

US OPEN CUP TITLES

1998, 2000, 2003, 2006

KEY PLAYERS

Chris Armas (1998–2007)
Robert Berić (2020–)
Cuauhtémoc Blanco (2007–09)
C. J. Brown (1998–2010)
Frank Klopas (1998–99)
Luboš Kubík (1998–2000)
Brian McBride (2008–10)
Piotr Nowak (1998–2002)
Ante Razov (1998–2000, 2001–04)
Bastian Schweinsteiger (2017–19)
Hristo Stoichkov (2000–02)
Zach Thornton (1998–2006)

KEY COACHES

Bob Bradley (1998–2002)
Dave Sarachan (2003–07)

MLS MOST VALUABLE PLAYER

Mike Magee (2013)

MLS DEFENDER OF THE YEAR

Luboš Kubík (1998)
Carlos Bocanegra (2002, 2003)

MLS GOALKEEPER OF THE YEAR

Jon Busch (2008)
Zach Thornton (1998)

MLS ROOKIE OF THE YEAR

Austin Berry (2012)
Carlos Bocanegra (2000)
Damani Ralph (2003)

MLS COMEBACK PLAYER OF THE YEAR

Chris Armas (2003)

MLS COACH OF THE YEAR

Bob Bradley (1998)
Dave Sarachan (2003)

GLOSSARY

assists
Passes that lead directly to goals.

double
In soccer, winning two important competitions—such as the MLS title and the US Open Cup—in the same season.

dynasty
A team that has an extended period of success, usually winning multiple championships in the process.

expansion team
A new team that is added to an existing league.

extra time
Two 15-minute periods added to a game if the score is tied at the end of regulation.

golden goal
A goal scored in extra time to win a game under a sudden-death format.

retired
Ended one's career.

rookie
A professional athlete in his or her first year of competition.

semifinal
The second-to-last round of play in a tournament; the winner of a semifinal game advances to the championship.

shutout
A game in which a team does not score.

striker
A player whose primary responsibility is to create scoring chances and score goals.

veteran
An athlete who has played many years.

MORE
INFORMATION

BOOKS

Kortemeier, Todd. *Total Soccer*. Minneapolis, MN: Abdo Publishing, 2017.

Marthaler, Jon. *Ultimate Soccer Road Trip*. Minneapolis, MN: Abdo Publishing, 2019.

Trusdell, Brian. *Soccer Record Breakers*. Minneapolis, MN: Abdo Publishing, 2016.

ONLINE RESOURCES

Booklinks
NONFICTION NETWORK
FREE! ONLINE NONFICTION RESOURCES

To learn more about Chicago Fire FC, please visit **abdobooklinks.com** or scan this QR code. These links are routinely monitored and updated to provide the most current information available.

INDEX

ABOUT THE AUTHOR

Anthony K. Hewson has followed American soccer since before the MLS days. Originally from San Diego, he now lives in the Bay Area with his wife and dogs.